CASPAR DAVID FRIEDRICH

*His
Life and Work*

CASPAR DAVID FRIEDRICH
IN HIS STUDIO.   About 1812.

Georg Friedrich Kersting
Nationalgalerie, Berlin

CASPAR DAVID FRIEDRICH

His
Life and Work

GERMAN LIBRARY OF INFORMATION

NEW YORK, N. Y.

1940

"*There are inner chambers in the history of the German spirit to which only its art history has the keys.*"

—Georg Dehio

INTRODUCTION

Recent researches in American cultural history have revealed how deeply the mystic philosophy of the German Romantic School permeated American life and thought in the second quarter of the Nineteenth Century. Emerson, Thoreau, Alcott, Channing and Bryant translated Schelling's *Naturphilosophie* and Kant's idealism into American Transcendentalism.

But curiously enough the embodiment of the Romantic attitude towards life, as it was expressed in the fine arts, that is to say in the landscape paintings of Caspar David Friedrich, escaped the attention of the poets and philosophers of the Transcendental School as it has, for that matter, to this day escaped the attention of all but a few enthusiasts and specialists in Germany's cultural history. This is the more to be wondered at in view of the fact that the subjective landscape has been a dominant tradition in American art and that it was Caspar David Friedrich who led the way in interpreting the landscape as a medium for subjective experience.

The one hundredth anniversary of Caspar David Friedrich's death offers an opportunity for paying tribute to his memory by means of acquainting a wider audience of American art lovers with the quality and scope of his work. For not only is Caspar David Friedrich the apotheosis of the Romantic idealism but he is a medium through which we may come in contact with one of the most constant and characteristic expressions of the German spirit.

It is for these reasons that the German Library of Information takes particular pleasure in presenting to the American public this brief outline of his life and work, the first of its kind to be published in this country.

GERMAN LIBRARY OF INFORMATION.

Dr. Matthias Schmitz

TABLE OF REPRODUCTIONS

CASPAR DAVID FRIEDRICH

"To romanticize is to give the ordinary and everyday a nobler meaning, the known the distinction of the unknown, the finite the aura of the infinite."

NOVALIS

"With words we may dominate the entire universe—only for the invisible, which is all about us, are words insufficient. But two other languages exist by means of which it is possible to express the divine. Only God can use one of these wondrous languages . . . the other is spoken by that chosen few whom He has annointed as His beloved among men—I mean Nature and Art."

WACKENRODER

"The landscape should be used as a veil through which one may glimpse a loftier reality."

SCHELLING

"Nature will be the medium through which the new art shall represent man's spiritual life."

RUNGE

With prophesies and theories such as these, the philosophers, critics, and seers of the Romantic Movement prepared the way for the Romantic landscape which was to be Germany's most significant and native contribution to Nineteenth Century painting. These theories and prophesies attained their first actuality in the landscapes of Caspar David Friedrich—landscapes which, for all their careful observation of nature, are permeated with a mystical sense of the universe. Gothic ruins, the rainbow and the Northern Lights, the immensity of the ocean, twisted oak trees and meadows stretching to far horizons were signs and symbols with which he endeavored to express eternal truths and at the same time bring about a renewal of the German spirit. They have had this effect upon many, although his contemporaries for the most part repudiated his work, appreciating neither its beauty nor its spiritual significance. Only in recent years has Friedrich's true greatness been recognized and his place assured in the consciousness of the German people.

But although Friedrich's paintings exist for themselves as works of art, they are nevertheless so integral a part of the Romantic Movement as it developed in Germany during the first decade of the Nineteenth Century, that an appreciation of their distinctive quality is greatly enhanced by relating Friedrich and his work to their philosophical and historical background. Furthermore, Romanticism in the German interpretation of the term differs so fundamentally from the French and Latin concept that a clarification of these differences is another important requisite for a more comprehensive appreciation of his work.

According to Gustav Pauli,[1] whose chapter on "Romanticism" in Dehio's "History of German Art" provides an illuminating analysis of Romantic theory and expression, "Romanticism is Germanic and reached its purest expression in those territories which are freest from Roman colonization. Everything that is regarded as an essential aspect of the Romantic spirit—individualism, irrationalism, the mystic welding together of subject and object, the tendency to intermingle the arts, the longing for the far-away and the strange, the

SELF PORTRAIT, Crayon, 1810.   *Nationalgalerie, Berlin*

feeling for the infinite and the continuity of historic development — all these are characteristic of German Romanticism and so much so that their union remains unintelligible to the Latins. What is known as Romanticism in France has only its name in common with German Romanticism."

Professor Richard Benz[2] of Heidelberg, in his exhaustive study of Romanticism as a *Totale Bewegung* (Total Movement), makes the following comparisons between the German and Latin concepts: "Romanticism is the first purely German cultural conception that exists; a culture more truly and exclusively German than even the Gothic which encompassed all Europe and to which the various peoples only gave their individual nuances."

"In France, bloody realism and exaggerated adventure as opposed to Classic stylization were regarded as Romantic, excepting, of course, the cult of the ghostly and the macabre which derived from Hoffmann's Tales."

Professor Richard Hamann of Marburg makes a similar statement: "For the French the Romantic point of view was always a German affair. What was later known as Romanticism in France was historic Realism with local color."[3]

In Germany the Romantic School encompassed all the arts. Its exponents attempted to reach *"Das Ding an Sich"* which Kant had declared was unknowable. The Romanticists taught a new conception of beauty which was feeling, mood, and emotion. In order to find a means of expressing the infinite and the unknowable they invented the language of symbolism and broke down the barriers between the arts

THE CROSS IN THE MOUNTAINS. 1806   *Staatliche Gemäldegalerie, Dresden*

which Lessing had been at such pains to establish. They opposed all inherited traditions of form. They placed *Kunstgefuehl* above *Kunstverstand*. In painting, the symbol and the hieroglyph were used and in music the *leit motif*.[4]

Although in the history of literature and art the Romantic School represents a definite period[5] and a clearly defined group of poets, painters, critics, and philosophers — the poets and writers were Wackenroder, Kleist, Novalis, Tieck, Brentano, and Arnim; the philosophers were Fichte, Schelling, and Schleiermacher; the painters, Runge, Friedrich, Carus, Kersting, and Blechen—nevertheless, the Romantic *Weltanschauung* is a constant and recurrent strain in the history of the German spirit. Schlegel, recognizing it as such, went so far as to rechristen it Gothic.

As a matter of fact, in the realm of painting, which is the principal concern of this essay, it will be found that German artists have been predominantly mystical, emotional or romantic. German painters have seldom exemplified the "art for art's sake" point of view. It has rather been art for the sake of a philosophy of life—an attitude which the Latin concept of form rejects. Altdorfer expressed the German's mystical communion with nature in his magical landscape of the German forest. Albrecht Duerer was interested in the world of science and metaphysics. Romantic traces are found in Elsheimer's twilight landscapes and Friedrich in his *"beseelte Landschaften"* ("Spiritualized Landscapes"), was an exponent of transcendental idealism.

THE RUINED MONASTERY OF ELDENA. 1808.   *Nationalgalerie, Berlin*

It is no accident that Friedrich should have chosen nature as the symbol with which to express his spiritualized conception of the universe, nor, for that matter, that the Romantic Movement should have emphasized the *"Heilige Natur"* motif in its philosophy, music and poetry. In no other literature or music do nature and the forest occur with such frequency. One remembers the lyrics of Goethe, Uhland, Moericke, Tieck, and Eichendorf, Weber's *"Der Freischuetz"* and the forest motifs in Wagner's music dramas. This identification with nature was not merely a tenet of the Romantic School; it was an inherent German tradition and goes back to the dawn of history when the German tribes identified their Gods with the elements of nature and when the holy grove and the *Welt Esche* were symbols in the ritual of worship. Caspar David Friedrich's *"Erdleben"* pictures became the apotheosis of Romantic nature philosophy. *"Erdleben"* was the name by which Friedrich's friend and pupil Carl Gustav Carus preferred to designate Friedrich's landscapes, believing that "landscape" was too trivial and inaccurate a word to describe their spiritual content.[6]

Seen as a period in the sequence of cultural cycles, the Romantic Movement was a flowering or the rebirth of a native strain which had lain dormant under successive layers of imported cultures. More specifically it came as a reaction against the French influence of the Eighteenth Century and the Classic Revival. The latter had dominated German creative expression ever since Winckelmann[7] laid down the precept that the only way for the Germans to be truly themselves and truly great

GERMANIC CHIEFTAIN'S GRAVE IN SNOW. About 1807.   *Gemäldegalerie, Dresden*

was to imitate the Greeks and the Romans. Acting on this precept, a generation of artists had journeyed to Rome to model themselves on Classic concepts of beauty. Then, at the turn of the century, a remarkable change occurred which gave the arts a new direction. As Ludwig Justi describes it, "the state robes of the French century are discarded and the true German quality reappears in deepest accord with the time of Duerer. A deep religious spirit rejects the cold intellectualism and clever sophistries of the Age of Reason."[8] A belief in the continuity of national tradition and its corollary, patriotism, were the other dominant characteristics of the new direction.

Wackenroder was the apostle of the movement.[9] In his *"Herzensergiessungen eines kunstliebenden Kloster-Bruders"*, a slender little volume which set down the artistic enthusiasm of a young monk, but which in reality reflected those of the author, the revolutionary idea was advanced that the German tradition in art had been neglected. Wackenroder pays homage to Albrecht Duerer who, according to the standards of Weimar Classicism, did not meet the classic requirements of *"edle Einfalt und stille Groesse"* ("Noble simplicity and quiet majesty"). The dominant Classic school felt itself tottering when he set up as his credo: "It is not only beneath Italian skies, under majestic domes and Corinthian columns, that true art can thrive; it lives also under pointed arches, intricately decorated buildings and Gothic spires."[10]

RUEGEN LANDSCAPE WITH RAINBOW.   1809.

Staatliches Museum, Weimar

Wackenroder did not, however, make the mistake of setting up old German art as the sole source of inspiration. He paid special tribute to "the divine Raphael" and to the sincerity and religious fervor of the *quatrocento*, an enthusiasm which was instrumental in sending the Nazarenes to Italy.[11]   It was, however, Wackenroder's belief in the divine mission of art—-"*Bildersaele sollen Tempel sein*" ("Picture galleries should be temples")—plus his revaluation of native tradition, which made him the apostle of the new school.

Wackenroder makes use of the term "Hieroglyph". "*Die Kunst redet durch Bilder der Menschen und bedienet sich also einer Hieroglyphenschrift*".   (Art speaks through man-made pictures and so makes use of a kind of hieroglyphic).

Later Runge and Wilhelm Schlegel used this term to describe the special type of symbol which would most effectively express Romantic ideology.   Friedrich on the other hand made infinite space and nature his symbols.[12]

At the turn of the century Dresden was the center of the Romantic Movement.   "Landscape" was the magical word. Tieck, the close friend of Wackenroder, Brentano, Novalis, and Schlegel, dreamed of allegorical landscapes which should surpass anything that had been done before.   Schelling lectured on *Naturphilosophie* at Jena and influenced not only the Romanticists but even that arch-Classicist, Goethe. Sternbald, the hero of Tieck's novel "*Franz Sternbalds Wanderungen*", which, in its pæans to old German art, supplements the "*Herzensergiessungen*", exclaims "Oh, my friend! If I could but translate into painting the heavenly music which

MONASTERY ELDENA IN WINTER.   1819.   *Nationalgalerie, Berlin*

the heavens are singing!" Philipp Otto Runge declared that the landscape was the new direction which the art of the Nineteenth Century would take.

It was into this ferment of creative ideas that Caspar David Friedrich, the blond young mystic from the North Sea, arrived in 1778. Justi describes him as *"Ein Meer-Kind, hellblond mit grossen, fragend-forschenden Augen."*[13] Son of a deeply religious father and feeling within himself that dedication to both nature and art which was the essence of Romantic philosophy, it was inevitable that he should have been drawn to its fountainhead. We know that in a short time he was to become the foremost exponent of Romantic ideology in the realm of the fine arts.

Caspar David Friedrich was born in Greifswald, Pomerania, September 5, 1774. His father was a soap and candle-maker and the descendant of an old Silesian family who had been forced to flee their lands during the Thirty Years' War. Because his talent evidenced itself at an early age he was permitted to take drawing lessons from Gottfried Quisdorp, instructor of drawing at the University of Greifswald. Quisdorp had been a pupil of Anton Graff, Germany's most prolific Eighteenth Century portrait painter. Within the limits of a dry style, Graff was an able technician with an amazing gift for accurate characterization.

In the autumn of 1794, Caspar David Friedrich entered the Academy of Copenhagen, which at this time ranked with the Academies of Dresden and Vienna. In addition to the sound academic training which the Academy provided, he

PORTRAIT OF CASPAR DAVID FRIEDRICH   *Nationalgalerie, Berlin*
—By Caroline Bardua. 1811.

must inevitably have come in contact with Romantic theory. Copenhagen was the center of northern Pietism and a colony of the Romantic School. Heinrich Steffens[14] had gone from Copenhagen to Germany to preach one of the basic tenets of Romantic philosophy—the continuity of national development—and to call upon the Germans to set an example to all free people that the nations should develop themselves in accordance with their inherited national traditions. Although the training afforded by the Academy could not have provided much of an incentive for the development of Romantic ideas, nevertheless it is significant that it produced the two greatest exponents of Romantic painting—Caspar David Friedrich and Philipp Otto Runge. Runge, also a North German—he was born at Wollgast—entered the Academy two years after Friedrich. It is probable that their early contact with the then fermenting Romantic ideas and the influence of their northern environment made these two artists less susceptible to the Classic and Latin influence than were those who journeyed to Rome.

Willoughby[15] reminds us that an overwhelming number of the pioneers and poets of Romanticism—Boehme, Hamann, Herder, Wackenroder, Tieck, Kleist, Hoffmann, Mueller, Fouqué, Arnim—were natives of the land east of the Elbe. Brandenburg, Silesia, Pomerania, East Prussia—these, he claims, are the cradle of Romantic mysticism in Germany.

In 1798, Friedrich enrolled in the Academy of Dresden, staying there for only a year although he returned again in 1802 to spend the remainder of his life in the Saxon capital. But

BOHEMIAN LANDSCAPE. Between 1815 and 1820

this year was an important one for his future development. Not only did he come in closer contact with the esthetics of the young movement, but he also had the opportunity of studying in the Dresden Gallery the methods and points of view exemplified in the work of the great baroque landscape painters, Poussin and Ruysdael. In spite of the invaluable lessons in construction and technique which they taught him, nevertheless the most significant effect was to turn him away from landscape used as a medium for a realistic presentation of reality or an ordered design, to a conception which should express his mystic subjective sense of the universe.

Returning to Greifswald, Friedrich commenced his studies of nature, which were to serve him as a repository of motifs in later years. He spent long days wandering through the oak forests and along the shores and cliffs of his beloved Ruegen. A favorite haunt was the ruined monastery at Eldena, built in the thirteenth century by Cistercian monks and destroyed during the Thirty Years' War. Like Wackenroder, he intrinsically sensed the beauty of North Gothic architecture and he made countless drawings of the monastery's arches and arcades. Gothic ruins, as we shall see, became a recurrent motif in his pictures, their reality based on the accurate studies made at this time.

Back at Dresden in 1802, Friedrich at first confined his efforts to the sepia wash drawings which were the fashion of the time and by the sale of which he was able to support himself. His first public recognition came through a sepia drawing of Ruegen which won the prize in a yearly competi-

CROSS IN THE RIESENGEBIRGE. 1811.   *Schloss Museum, Berlin*

tion sponsored by the Weimar Friends of Art in the Propylaeen. This brought Friedrich to the attention of Goethe who gave the drawing a favorable review in the Jenaische Allgemeine Literatur Schriften. Although Goethe did not follow Friedrich in his more transcendental phases, he was always ready to lend a helping hand. It was upon Goethe's advice that the Grand Duke of Saxe-Weimar purchased the "Landscape with Rainbow" and the collection of sepia drawings which are now in the State Museum at Weimar. It was not, however, until the following year, 1806, that Friedrich essayed oil painting and so commenced finding himself as the exponent of *"die unendliche Landschaft"* ("The Infinite Landscape").

The young Countess of Thun had seen a drawing in Friedrich's studio which had deeply moved her; a solitary cross raised high above a lonely mountain peak, illuminated by the last rays of the evening sun. She asked Friedrich to execute a similar subject in color for her house chapel at Tetschen. Hence the name *"Der Tetschner Altar"* which, in listings of Friedrich's work, frequently supplements the title *"Kreuz im Gebirge"* ("Cross in the Mountains"). The painting is now in the Friedrich Gallery in the State Museum at Dresden. This and the "Landscape with Rainbow" are Friedrich's most popular and most widely-reproduced pictures.

Today there does not seem to be much ground for the discussion, much of it unfavorable, that this picture aroused. It might have been an accidental motif taken from nature, had its religious purpose not been clearly designated by the

SOLITARY TREE. 1823.   *Nationalgalerie, Berlin*

heavy gold frame on which were carved symbols of Christianity. In spite of the deep reverence which permeates the picture it was described as "heathenish"—possibly because Friedrich dared to replace the traditional holy picture with a landscape. The placing of the cross in a landscape should be interpreted as a profession of Friedrich's faith—meaning that for him the soul of nature was as much a subject for reverence as the symbol of Christianity. It embodied the Romanticist reverence for the *"Weltseele"*—the "Over Soul".

In 1810 Friedrich sent two large canvases to the Berlin Academy which brought him increasing recognition and won him his election to that body. They were "Monk on the Sea Coast" and the "Ruined Monastery of Eldena in Winter". Both were bought by the Prussian Crown Prince and are to this day to be seen in the royal suite of the Berlin *Schloss Museum*. "The Ruined Monastery of Eldena" became a favorite and recurrent motif with Friedrich. A similar version of the Schloss "Ruin" is in the collection of the National Gallery, Berlin, where there is also an early realistic treatment of the same motif. The *Neue Pinakothek* had still another version which was burned in the Glas-Palast holocaust in 1931. It is the first time that Gothic churches, seen as ruins, appear in painting. In the preceding century ruins were a favorite device with which to augment the picturesque nostalgia for the past, but they were invariably Greek temples and crumbling Corinthian columns. The *"Kuenstliche Ruine"* ("Artificial Ruin"), was also a popular decorative device of Eighteenth Century landscape architects.

ASCENDING MISTS IN THE RIESENGEBIRGE. 1811.   *Staatsgemäldesammlung, Munich*

But in Friedrich's pictures the ruins are introduced because of their symbolism. The old faith is represented as a ruin and the new beliefs suggested by the evergreens which are springing up in their midst.

Walking tours in the Riesengebirge, which Friedrich took with his friend and fellow painter, Georg Kersting, furnished him with motifs for another group of landscapes. In 1812 he exhibited "The Cross in the Riesengebirge"—a picture which the Berlin Classicists, who named Friedrich the "Dresden Mystic", described as *"einfach greulich"* (simply horrible). But the King, *"der Romantiker am Throne"*, ("The Romanticist on the Throne") as he has been described, said of it, *"Das ist ein schoenes Bild"* (That is a nice picture), and straightway bought it. In refutation of its reputed lack of realism he said, *"As I traveled to Toplitz, I arose early in order to see the beautiful scenery. Out of the mist soared the high peaks and made exactly the effect of the surface of a sea. Who has not seen it in nature, would not believe it true."* Many people interpreted this picture, painted during the years of the Napoleonic domination, to mean the ultimate redemption of their Fatherland.

His friendship with the great Romantic dramatist, Heinrich von Kleist, and his own deep sense of the national humiliation inspired a series of political pictures. Kleist's "Hermannsschlacht", written in 1807, was a passionate summons to young Germany to throw off the Napoleonic yoke. Friedrich too, in his political pictures, hoped to bring about a regeneration of the German spirit. "The Tomb of Arminius",

THE ALPS. 1824.   *Nationalgalerie, Berlin*

churchyards showing graves of heroes, and a marine, *"Adler ueber Nebelmeer"* ("Eagle Flying Over a Sea of Mist"), which symbolized the emergence of the German spirit from political storms and mists, are some of the subjects. It is significant, however, that the political motifs were always used in conjunction with a landscape background.

Friedrich's symbolism was invariably more effective when he confined himself to pure landscape or introduced a figure or two into the foreground of his landscape compositions. But whether he paints mountain peaks rising above the mists, or the green distances of rolling meadows, the stillness of pine forests in winter, or the bare tangle of masts in the harbor at Greifswald—in all of them one senses the mysterious presence of eternity. When Friedrich introduced figures into his landscapes, they were never painted full face. but turned away from the beholder. Gazing into the distance they seem to share the emotion which the artist himself has felt. They are *"Doppelgaenger"* (a second self), who transmit the artist's emotion. Although Friedrich's pictures need no explanatory footnotes to convey their deep sincerity and profound spiritual content, nevertheless it is impressive to learn from his own diary and from those of his friends what were his esthetic beliefs and what were the technical methods he used to express them.

His fundamental principle was clearly and simply stated when he wrote: "If you desire to dedicate yourself to art, if you feel within yourself an inner compulsion to consecrate your life to art—Oh, then heed your inner voice, for it is the

GARDEN TERRACE. 1811.   *Schloss Museum, Berlin*

spirit of art within you; you must hold as sacred every pure emotion of your spirit; you must listen to every reverent thought for that is the art spirit within you. In the hour of inspiration it will assume a visible form and that form is your picture."[16]

According to Kersting and Carus none of Friedrich's pictures were painted from nature although he made careful studies of trees, rocks, and mountain formations. But once he had conceived his picture, he banished all sketches from his studio and worked directly from the promptings of the inner eye of the spirit.

In 1816, Friedrich was made a member of the Dresden Academy. This carried with it a small salary. In 1818 he was made Professor. A full Professorship, which he had hoped for, was never granted because it was felt that his painting was too personal, his point of view too individual to serve as a fruitful example to students.

We must think of Friedrich in these years as a shy recluse. The "most solitary of the solitary" his friends described him. It was therefore a great surprise when he married a young and penniless girl, Karoline Bommer, whom none of his friends had known. But marriage does not seem to have altered his life. He was still a solitary, and spent many hours of the day and night wandering through the woods and fields, frequently starting out before daylight — a strange companion for a young girl. And we sense something a little wistful and forlorn in the figure standing at a window, which he painted shortly after his marriage, using his wife

AT THE WINDOW.   About 1818   *Nationalgalerie, Berlin*

as a model.   It is the only interior which Friedrich is known
to have painted.   The figure is hardly a portrait of Karoline
since, in the true Friedrich tradition, her back is turned and
we follow her gaze as she looks out of the window at the Elbe
with its passing ships.

Friedrich's worldly success was short-lived and from
1820 until his death his pictures ceased to interest the public.   Kleist, who had done so much to interpret his work, was
dead and the Romantic movement as a whole was turning
away from its initial lofty idealism.[17] But in spite of his lack
of popular success, it is highly significant that the creative
spirits of his time recognized his true greatness.   Kleist,
Tieck, Novalis, Runge, Kersting, Carus, Dahl, Schinkel and
even Goethe, for all his disbelief in Romantic theory, were
his champions.

It is also significant that by far the largest number of
his patrons were members of the aristocracy; an indication,
according to Kurt Karl Eberlein, the Friedrich authority, that
the aristocracy were still arbiters of quality.[18] Among Friedrich's royal and aristocratic patrons were the King and Crown
Prince of Prussia, the Grand Duke of Saxe-Weimar, the
Czar of Russia, the Princes of the House of Wettin, Baron
Speck von Sternberg, Prince Putbus, and a score of others.
The Russian crown prince had once told Friedrich that if he
should ever be in need, he must not hesitate to call upon him
for assistance.   Friedrich accepted his offer when a stroke dis-
abled his right arm and he had been advised that it could only
be cured by treatments at Bad Terplitz. The necessary funds

SAND DUNES AT RUEGEN. About 1803. Water Color and Pencil.   *Nationalgalerie, Berlin*

were accomplished by the sale of a number of his pictures to the Russian royal family.

Posterity is indebted to Kersting, whose interiors with figures are among the most charming examples of Biedermeier Romanticism, for three portraits of Friedrich painted at the easel in his Dresden studio. Friedrich's brooding, melancholy gaze and the monk-like austerity of the room give us an unforgettable picture of the spiritual intensity and the negation of ordinary standards of comfort which characterized his life and his work. Into this monastic studio, Carus brought the French sculptor David D'Anger who had come to Germany in 1834 to do a series of portraits in relief of the outstanding poets and painters of the time. When Friedrich reluctantly showed him his canvases, D'Anger said, "Here is a man who has discovered the tragedy of the landscape."

Carus was a man of many accomplishments. Besides being a painter he was court physician, an eminent natural scientist, and a distinguished writer. His book, "Nine Letters on Landscape Painting" in which he outlines the problems and goal of Romantic landscape painting became programatic for the Romantic School. His precepts derived very largely from his study of Friedrich's works and his absorption of Friedrich's philosophy. In fact many of Carus's paintings are so much like his master's that, until the recent expertizing of Friedrich's work was undertaken, they frequently were mistaken for his. Friedrich never signed a picture, believing that

FAREWELL. 1818.

Formerly in the Ducal Museum at Gotha,
Burned in Glas-Palast Fire, 1931.

the picture should carry its own signature and that the artist must necessarily be recognized in his work.

Another one of Friedrich's staunchest supporters was the Norwegian painter, Johann Christian Claussen Dahl, who came to Dresden as professor of landscape painting at the Academy. He had seen the Constable exhibition in Paris and had brought to his teaching the new observation of light and air which was eventually to lead to Impressionism. Among the younger painters who came under Dahl's influence, there was a definite swing away from the romantic viewpoint to a more realistic observation of nature and to a greater interest in painting-quality as an end in itself. Dahl influenced Friedrich to a certain extent and there is a tendency towards a looser handling and a less elegiac mood in some of the landscapes of this period. Although Dahl's trend was towards realism he defended Friedrich against his detractors who regarded him as a self-conscious mystic. Dahl has described him as "one of the most original of artists and peculiar of men, whose like will not be seen again." Friedrich's landscape elegies, according to Dahl, represented "the mysterious life of the universe with a tragic mysticism. They are visions of the unknown world, profoundly and poetically expressed."

Friedrich never recovered entirely from his illness and during the last years of his life lapsed into a state of melancholy, rousing himself only occasionally to plan a new monumental version of the Eldena Ruin motif which, however, was never carried out. When he died, only a few recognized his significance, and even before his death, Carus had

THE HARBOR AT GREIFSWALD.
Between 1810 and 1815.

Formerly in the Collection
of the Kunsthalle, Hamburg
Burned in the Glas-Palast Fire in 1931

said "Friedrich is already forgotten" and commented on the curious fact that the entire period with which he was identified should so soon have become outmoded, pushed aside as it was by the ubiquitous influence of Duesseldorf Realism.

And Friedrich himself, commenting upon the public's disregard of his work, wrote in his diary shortly before his death: "I am not so weak or eager for fame that I can assume a style which does not grow from an inner conviction — and so I spin myself in my cocoon and shall let time decide what will emerge therefrom."

More than fifty years were to elapse before Friedrich's reputation emerged from the oblivion to which successive art epochs inimical to Romantic esthetics had relegated it.[19] To this day, he takes his place beside the noblest and most authentic purveyors of the German spirit.

It was the *"Jahrhundert"* Exhibition held in Berlin in 1906 which brought about Friedrich's rediscovery, as it also did that of a number of other forgotten Nineteenth Century painters.[20] The exhibition was arranged for the purpose of reacquainting the German people with the important contribution which their own artists had made to Nineteenth Century art and, in so doing, to counteract the recurrent tendency to regard France and Italy as the sources of all that was significant in the fine arts.

It was a curious swinging back of the pendulum to the point of view which had conditioned the Romantic School a century before. During the first decade of the Twentieth Century, German art historians commenced occupying them-

AGES OF MAN. Before 1815.

Museum der Bildenden Kuenste, Leipzig

selves with problems of German form and the continuity of a German tradition in the fine arts. Dehio, Woelfflin, Woeringer, Lichtwark, Pauli and Tschudi were among the historians and museum directors who demonstrated by means of histories and exhibitions the characteristics of German form and the continuity of a German tradition — a tradition which had persisted despite recurrent waves of Classic and Latin influence. In establishing this continuity, Romantic painting, as an expression of an essentially and peculiarly Germanic point of view, was rescued from the discard of outmoded art periods to which francophile critics had relegated it.

The Friedrich revival commenced at this time and with it the beginnings of the important collections of his work which are to be seen at Berlin, Hamburg, Dresden and Munich. Today, every art museum in Germany has its Romantic collection which boasts at least one Caspar David Friedrich; and for the last fifteen years museums and galleries have vied with each other in holding comprehensive surveys of Romantic paintings and graphic arts. When eight Friedrichs were burned in the Glas-Palast fire of 1931, where a special loan exhibition of Romantic paintings was being held, the press treated it as nothing less than a national catastrophe.

If one accepts the hypothesis that every significant art expression develops its distinctive style and form, then it would seem as if the Romantic School does not meet the test. For there is no distinctive Romantic style; merely a Romantic point of view. Both Runge and Friedrich employed the linear

CHALK CLIFFS AT RUEGEN.   About 1820.   *Reinhardt Collection, Winterthur*

style of late Eighteenth Century Classicism. But, nevertheless, it is undeniable that their work is highly personal and filled with an impressive mysticism which differentiates it from the Classic school. Before German Romantic painting can be appreciated to its full extent by art lovers steeped in the "art for art's sake" tradition it is necessary to accept another hypothesis, namely that there can be two standards of art.

But for those to whom poetic content is important — who require that painting as well as poetry should reveal and interpret eternal truths — for them Friedrich needs no explanation or introduction. His landscapes have that "impassioned contemplation" which is the essence and aim of the poetic spirit.

TWO MEN IN CONTEMPLATION OF THE MOON. 1819.   *Gemäldegalerie, Dresden*

NOTES

The following is the original German text of the quotations on page 11.

"Romantisieren ist dem Gemeinen einen hohen Sinn geben, dem Bekannten die Würde des Unbekannten, dem Endlichen einen unendlichen Schein."
—NOVALIS

"Durch Worte herrschen wir über den ganzen Erdkreis . . . Nur das Unsichtbare, das über uns schwebt, ziehen Worte nicht in unser Gemüt herab. Es gibt aber zwei andere Sprachen, durch welche uns vergönnt ist die Himmlischen Dinge mit ganzer Macht zu fassen und zu begreifen. . . . Die eine dieser wundervollen Sprachen redet nur Gott; die andere reden nur wenige Auserwählte unter den Menschen, die er zu seinen Lieblingen gesalbt hat. Ich meine: die Natur und die Kunst."—WACKENRODER

"Sinn der Landschaft ist es, die Dinge als eine Hülle zu gebrauchen, die eine höhere Art von Wahrscheinlichkeit durchscheinen lasse.—SCHELLING

"Die neue Kunst soll den Menschen, das heisst seine Seele, in welcher sein Zusammenhang mit Gott gegeben ist, sein seelisches Leben durch die Natur darstellen."—RUNGE

(1) Gustav Pauli, in Dehio's "Geschichte der Deutschen Kunst," Vol. 4, Das Neunzehnte Jahrhundert. 1934.

(2) Richard Benz, Professor of Art at Heidelberg. "Die Deutsche Romantik". 1937.

(3) Richard Hamann, Professor of Art at the University of Marburg, "Geschichte der Kunst". 1935.

(4) L. A. Willoughby, "The Romantic Movement in Germany", 1932.

(5) The Storm and Stress period of German literature was a forerunner of German Romanticism because of its emphasis on individualism and because of its defiance of accepted rules. However, the emotional and somewhat sensational realism of Schiller's "Die Räuber" and Goethe's "Sorrows of Werther" had little in common with the transcendental idealism of the Romantic School.

(6) Gustav Carus "Neun Briefe über Landschaftsmalerei". 1815-24. Carus describes subjective landscape painting as "Erdlebenbildkunst".

(7) Johann Joachim Winckelmann, 1717—1768, was the great German archæologist and historian who was "destined to assert and interpret the charm of the Hellenic spirit", as Walter Pater describes his mission, and whose summation of the essence of classic art—"Edle Einfalt und Stille Grösse"—noble simplicity and quiet grandeur—became the standard of the Classic Revival.

(8)   Ludwig Justi, "Von Runge bis Thoma", 1932.

(9)   "Outpourings from the Heart of an Art Loving Monk", Wilhelm Heinrich Wackenroder, 1773-1798. "His uncanny and impressionable receptivity, his childlike religious fervor, his moral and artistic temperament made him the real inspirer of Romanticism". Richard Benz, "Die Deutsche Romantik", 1937.

(10) Although in 1773 Goethe had written a pæan to Erwin von Steinbach, the architect of the Strassburg Cathedral, which was contained in Herder's, "Von deutscher Art und Kunst", nevertheless he was at heart a fervent admirer of Classic art.

(11) In the "Gemäldebeschreibungen aus Paris", 1802-04, Schlegel had recognized the practical difficulty of expressing Romantic concepts with their emphasis on religious content, in terms of the hieroglyph or allegory. He realized also that it was difficult for the artists to bring art back to its old significance unless based on tradition. He therefore advanced the idea that religious content could be best expressed by using religious subjects and by recapturing the religious fervor of the *quatrocento*. These ideas were put into practice by a group of painters known as the Nazarenes who went to Rome to saturate themselves in the method and spirit of the Italian Primitives. In so doing these artists repudiated one of the basic tenets of Romanticism—the reviving of a national art deriving from a national tradition.

(12) In "Die Gemälde", a dialogue published in the Athenæum (1799) Wilhelm Schlegel claimed that a painting was a "divine symbol, a hieroglyph" and in another instance he asked "how is it possible to bring the infinite to the surface and give it visible form? Only through symbols, images and signs."
      Runge asserted that the new Romantic painting would lead to the use of the arabesque and the hieroglyph, but that from this the landscape would result. See Richard Benz "Die Deutsche Romantik".

(13) "A blond child of the sea, with great questioning, searching eyes."

(14) H. Heinrich Steffens, 1773—1845, German philosopher of Norwegian extraction, a friend of Schelling's and Schleiermacher's. Lectured at Copenhagen, fought on German side against Napoleon. Taught at Breslau and Berlin.

(15) Herder, without whom Romanticism was unthinkable, had declared that the salvation of the modern world lay in taking up the thread of continuous national development where it had been broken at the Renaissance. Willoughby, "The Romantic Movement in Germany". 1932.

(16) "Willst du dich der Kunst widmen, fühlst du inneren Beruf, ihr dein Leben zu weihen, oh, so achte auf die Stimme deines Innern; . . . . Heilig sollst du halten jede reine Regung deines Gemütes; heilig achten jede fromme Ahnung; denn sie ist Kunst in uns. In begeisternder Stunde wird sie zur anschaulichen Form, und diese Form ist dein Bild."
—Caspar David Friedrich

(17) A second generation of Romantic painters had developed whose work was more understandable and therefore more popular.   Ludwig Richter headed the school of so-called Biedermeier Romanticism which painted the life of the small town Bürger with idyllic charm, another group developed the "Ritter-Romantik", which used romantic mediæval tales for its motives and still another group painted the German landscape with exaggerated picturesqueness using woodland scenes reminiscent of the "Wolfenschlucht" in "Der Freischütz".

(18) Karl Kurt Eberlein: "Die Weltkunst", May 1940, "Friedrich und die Sammler".

(19) In his exhaustive "History of 19th Century Painting", 1890, Muther dismisses Friedrich with six lines and Meier-Gräfe in his "Modern Painting" 1907, makes no mention of Friedrich, although he discusses Richter and Schwind as exponents of 19th century German Romanticism.

(20) Jahrhundert (Centennial) Exhibition, covering the hundred years between 1775 and 1875. Such portrait painters as von Rayski, Ammerling, Wassman and Spector, the Biedermeier Romanticists Kersting, Richter, Schwind and Spitzweg and Friedrich's great contemporary Runge were among the artists whom the exhibition rediscovered.

M H

DATE DUE	
APR 2 1 1997	
May 6, 1997	
OCT 0 6 1998	
OCT 27 1998	
MAR 1 2 2014	